Thoughts and Imaginings

By Peche

ISBN: 1540882632
ISBN-13: 978-1540882639

THOUGHTS

IMAGININGS

THOUGHTS

IMAGININGS

THOUGHTS

IMAGININGS

THOUGHTS

IMAGININGS

THOUGHTS

IMAGININGS

THOUGHTS

IMAGININGS

THOUGHTS

IMAGININGS

THOUGHTS

IMAGININGS

THOUGHTS

IMAGININGS

THOUGHTS

IMAGININGS

THOUGHTS

IMAGININGS

THOUGHTS

IMAGININGS

THOUGHTS

IMAGININGS

THOUGHTS

IMAGININGS

THOUGHTS

IMAGININGS

THOUGHTS

IMAGININGS

THOUGHTS

IMAGININGS

THOUGHTS

IMAGININGS

THOUGHTS

IMAGININGS

THOUGHTS

IMAGININGS

THOUGHTS

IMAGININGS

THOUGHTS

IMAGININGS

THOUGHTS

IMAGININGS

THOUGHTS

IMAGININGS

THOUGHTS

IMAGININGS

THOUGHTS

IMAGININGS

THOUGHTS

IMAGININGS

THOUGHTS

IMAGININGS

THOUGHTS

IMAGININGS

THOUGHTS

IMAGININGS

THOUGHTS

IMAGININGS

THOUGHTS

IMAGININGS

THOUGHTS

IMAGININGS

THOUGHTS

IMAGININGS

THOUGHTS

IMAGININGS

THOUGHTS

IMAGININGS

THOUGHTS

IMAGININGS

THOUGHTS

IMAGININGS

THOUGHTS

IMAGININGS

THOUGHTS

IMAGININGS

THOUGHTS

IMAGININGS

THOUGHTS

IMAGININGS

THOUGHTS

IMAGININGS

THOUGHTS

IMAGININGS

THOUGHTS

IMAGININGS

THOUGHTS

IMAGININGS

THOUGHTS

IMAGININGS

THOUGHTS

IMAGININGS

THOUGHTS

IMAGININGS

THOUGHTS

IMAGININGS

THOUGHTS

IMAGININGS

THOUGHTS

IMAGININGS

THOUGHTS

IMAGININGS

THOUGHTS

IMAGININGS

THOUGHTS

IMAGININGS

THOUGHTS

IMAGININGS

THOUGHTS

IMAGININGS

THOUGHTS

IMAGININGS

THOUGHTS

IMAGININGS

THOUGHTS

IMAGININGS

THOUGHTS

IMAGININGS

THOUGHTS

IMAGININGS

THOUGHTS

IMAGININGS

THOUGHTS

IMAGININGS

THOUGHTS

IMAGININGS

THOUGHTS

IMAGININGS

THOUGHTS

IMAGININGS

THOUGHTS

IMAGININGS

THOUGHTS

IMAGININGS

THOUGHTS

IMAGININGS

THOUGHTS

IMAGININGS

THOUGHTS

IMAGININGS

THOUGHTS

IMAGININGS

THOUGHTS

IMAGININGS

THOUGHTS

IMAGININGS

THOUGHTS

IMAGININGS

THOUGHTS

IMAGININGS

THOUGHTS

IMAGININGS

THOUGHTS

IMAGININGS

THOUGHTS

IMAGININGS

THOUGHTS

IMAGININGS

THOUGHTS

IMAGININGS

THOUGHTS

IMAGININGS

THOUGHTS

IMAGININGS

THOUGHTS

IMAGININGS

THOUGHTS

IMAGININGS

THOUGHTS

IMAGININGS

THOUGHTS

IMAGININGS

THOUGHTS

IMAGININGS

THOUGHTS

IMAGININGS

THOUGHTS

IMAGININGS

THOUGHTS

IMAGININGS

THOUGHTS

IMAGININGS

THOUGHTS

IMAGININGS

THOUGHTS

IMAGININGS

THOUGHTS

IMAGININGS

THOUGHTS

IMAGININGS

THOUGHTS

IMAGININGS

THOUGHTS

IMAGININGS

THOUGHTS

IMAGININGS

THOUGHTS

IMAGININGS

THOUGHTS

IMAGININGS

THOUGHTS

IMAGININGS

THOUGHTS

IMAGININGS

THOUGHTS

IMAGININGS

THOUGHTS

IMAGININGS

THOUGHTS

IMAGININGS

THOUGHTS

IMAGININGS

THOUGHTS

IMAGININGS

THOUGHTS

IMAGININGS

THOUGHTS

IMAGININGS

THOUGHTS

IMAGININGS

THOUGHTS

IMAGININGS

THOUGHTS

IMAGININGS

THOUGHTS

IMAGININGS

THOUGHTS

IMAGININGS

THOUGHTS

IMAGININGS

THOUGHTS

IMAGININGS

THOUGHTS

IMAGININGS

www.ingramcontent.com/pod-product-compliance
Lightning Source LLC
Chambersburg PA
CBHW071418180526
45170CB00001B/142
9781540882639